ENGLISH

COUNTRY TRADITIONS

ENGLISH
COUNTRY TRADITIONS

WOOD ENGRAVINGS BY

CHRISTOPHER WORMELL

———

WRITTEN BY

IAN NIALL

PAVILION

This edition published in Great Britain in 1990 by
PAVILION BOOKS LIMITED
196 Shaftesbury Avenue, London WC2H 8JL

Text copyright © Ian Niall
Illustrations copyright © Christopher Wormell

Designed by John Gorham

A CIP catalogue record for this book is
available from the British Library

ISBN 1 85145 5167

Printed in Great Britain by Butler & Tanner Ltd
Frome and London

10 9 8 7 6 5 4 3 2 1

CONTENTS

FOREWORD

Christopher Wormell has been active as a wood engraver for little more than five years. In that time he has not only established himself as a master in the medium but also made a place for it in contemporary graphics as a force to be reckoned with. Son of a landscape painter he left school at 18 in 1973 to support himself in a variety of jobs while devoting himself to painting. He has always greatly admired the work of the father of the English wood engraving tradition, Thomas Bewick (1753-1828), whose blocks he remembered seeing as a child in the V & A. In 1982, visits to the exhibition of work by Reynolds Stone (1900-1979) in the National Art Library at the V & A confirmed his resolution to develop his interest in a medium then generally considered in terms of its historic achievements.

There can be no doubt that wood engraving enjoyed a revival in the mid-1980s, one that continues unabated today. We see it in the activities of the Society of Wood Engravers, established in 1920 by Robert Gibbings, Noel Rooke, Eric Gill and others, which seemed to draw increasing attention to itself after the arrival of Hilary Paynter in 1984. Christopher Wormell's career testifies to the same revival of interest. His first work as an engraver was for Faber & Faber, a book cover for Brian Friel's play *The Communication Cord*, followed by a design for Seamus Heaney poems and other commissions. Perhaps what really launched Christopher Wormell's work was the series of illustrations he provided for the series 'British Cookery' in the *Observer* newspaper's colour magazine early in 1984. Today he can look back on a series of commissions done for an impressively wide range of clients, from Jonathan Cape and Penguin to the *Radio Times*, *The Times*, Goldcrest Films, David Puttnam and Saatchi and Saatchi.

Christopher Wormell is evidently most at home when providing illustrations for a text published in a book. He had long admired the writings of Ian Niall before meeting him in the winter of 1985-6 to discuss the work published in the following pages. Wormell followed his mentors Bewick and Stone in reserving his best work for the English landscape. Who more suitable than Niall, author of *The Poacher's Handbook* and *A Galloway Childhood*, to say nothing of the *Portrait of a Country Artist* commemorating his friend Charles Tunnicliffe, to provide texts from which the wood engraver could take his cue.

ELIZABETH ESTEVE-COLL
DIRECTOR OF THE VICTORIA AND ALBERT MUSEUM, 1988

T IS NOT RECORDED that Adam kept bees in the Garden of Eden but man has indeed kept bees for a very long time treating them with less respect than the modern up-to-date apiarist when, to steal the honey, he did not hesitate to destroy his colony. The drone of the bee is synonymous with high summer in the clover field, sunshine blessing the lime tree, and charlock growing to add contrast to the green of the rising corn or the root field. The urgency of honey-gathering shortens the lives of foraging bees while countless new wax cells are built to accommodate honey, nectar and pollen, the 'bread' of the colony. Beyond the work of stocking up for the winter there are other important duties members of the colony perform – ventilating the hive on hot days, cleaning the premises, guarding against intruders, nursing the young, feeding the queen, and, when the need arises, dying in battle against invading wasps or large bumble bees. There is surely no more perfectly ordered society than we find in the hive.

The townsman is less likely to be able to accommodate a beehive on his premises, but since time immemorial the cottager has kept bees. Looking after apiaries was part of the labour of monks. The Romans were advised on the management of bees by the poet, Virgil, and honey has always been credited with wonderful healing properties as well as having great benefit to the person who takes it by the spoonful to soothe a cough.

Today, few mysteries concerning the life of the bee remain unsolved. The humblest cottager when he goes to 'take the honey off' knows from books just what the system he is disturbing is all about, but the taste of honey depends on the season. If there was an early spring and a great abundance of blossom the beekeeper may taste honey that came from the apple tree overlaid, perhaps, with sycamore and a touch of the field maple. Later his honey, if he lives within reach of moorland, will be dark and heavy, a gathering from ling and heather.

Order came to the keeping of bees when men who knew how to harness the colony to their needs designed beehives with queen excluders that confined the queen to what is known as the 'brood chamber' in which she would lay her eggs. The worker bees, smaller in girth, could hurry up above and store food there in frames built in higher blocks. By examining the progress of honey gathering the cottager can decide for himself when it is time to take his honey. He never dares take it all unless he is prepared to replace it with a gallon or two of sugar either in liquid form or candy. Honey has the same quality as wine. It never can be exactly the same again because that precise sequence of summer days will never be repeated.

Beehives

HERE HAS ALWAYS BEEN a tendency to conjure up a romantic picture of the reaper in the rye grass. Hay had always been both feed and bedding for livestock when other things, straw and bracken, weren't freely available. Before the hay baler and the Cubist scene of the modern hayfield – men and women, casually using hayrakes and long-handled hayforks, gathered in the first important harvest of the year.

With the enchantment of nostalgia, it was all a kind of picnic under a heavenly sky and the twittering flights of swallow and martin high above it all. God was in his heaven when, on the hay scented field, butterflies settled to sun themselves and the grasshopper sang endlessly. Such idylls are made of fond memory of the heat haze and happy, laughing people lounging after their labours by the tea basket. They were always surrounded by wild snapdragons, meadowsweet that was almost over-powering in its sweetness, and delicate hairbells that swayed in the gentle breeze. Time was marked by thistledown sailing silently up, and away.

The truth, reality, was something quite different. The hay-maker listened for the rumble of distant thunder and looked anxiously for the rain cloud. A downpour meant that all his labour would be undone. The gathered swath would have to be forked or raked apart again. In its wet state it was fatal to build hay into a haycock. It couldn't be carted into the rickyard or the barn. When the expected rain cloud came crawling across the countryside the whole process of hay-making went back to its beginning.

'Tomorrow and tomorrow' – the Bard might have been writing those immortal lines about hay-making, for the raking and turning would go on day after day, week after week. It wasn't the picnic that kept the peasant family working in the field but sheer desperation. It could all be made worse by biting insects and the awful irritation when small seeds worked their way down into a man's heavy woollen vest. In that long-dreaded moment when the first raindrops began to spatter down, long-bodied rainflies emerged from the ditch to settle on the team of horses and sometimes on the exposed arms and chests of the haymakers themselves to drink blood and inflict severe pain. After a little while it would all become unbearable as well as futile, even if the first few cooling moments of the rain increased the lovely perfume from the nearby beanfield and the honeysuckle in the hedge. If the tang of swedes revived the weary, the truth was that a hayfield had never been a place for anyone who couldn't go on, but had to lie on his back while the sun shone and he admired that sheepflock of far-up white clouds.

Hay-making

VERYONE WHO HAS ever gone mushrooming learns that some fields are better than others, while some never have a mushroom on them. The old countryman knows even more – those places he harvests year after year. His special field is a most closely guarded secret. He is careful to pick it bare so that not a single cluster of mushrooms remains to advertise what a latecomer might expect if he could force himself to leave his bed early enough and venture forth into the dawn. Long before the traffic has begun to destroy the holy peace of early morning, the mushroomer who knows his business is out and back home again with mushrooms tastier than anything the professional grower can ever hope to produce in his dark barn or basement.

The field that grows the real mushroom is one long lain fallow or never ploughed at all. It is an ancient pasture of rich, deep turf that ponies have grazed, a place sheltered a little from the fiercest of the sun's heat in an Indian summer, if such a late summer there has been. In the rich loam in which the wholesome grass roots find nourishment spores of the fungus have fallen. The tracery of mycelium, branching again and again, and more beautiful than the most delicate work of the lace-maker, spreads and gives rise, quite literally, to the mushroomer's breakfast feast. The common field mushroom, alas, is where the average mushroom gatherer draws his line, although both fields and woods abound in similar delicacies, some less appetising than the great horse mushroom that stains the gravy black, and others, like the morel and the blusher, highly prized by the expert chef.

Why then is it that country folk are so conservative in their taste? Unfortunately the pastures and woodlands that support the growth of such delicacies as the chanterelle and St George's mushroom also produce the fly agaric and the angel of death. Death from eating the dangerous toadstools is less likely than it is from eating some of the funguses that bear a resemblance to the commoner, edible sorts. Nature seems to have contrived to give the death cap, and others like it, a forbidding colour and shape. A few, like the sickener, teach those with a too catholic taste not to take too much for granted. The result is that many of the edible fungi abounding in the fields and woods in autumn remain unharvested. A squirrel eats them. Perhaps even the fox, with a more resilient constitution and a stronger stomach, samples them. The puffball is often left to brown and explode in a pepper dust at the touch of a boot. Boys kick the giant puffball like a football, but in a few short weeks all wilt and die.

Wild Mushrooms

IT MIGHT BE suggested that long ago, when the horse plough was in the mind of the man who subsequently invented it, the blacksmith looked up and took inspiration from the design he saw in the pattern of the stars in the north. Now, alas, the horse-drawn plough is an obsolete implement, and the great horses that pulled it are redundant. Neither the plough nor the ploughman will ever again inspire our nature poets as they did. Burns, Gray and Housman – who could find inspiration in a plough that fouls the morning air with diesel fumes while its operator sits in a perspex cabin and operates the lever that enables the ugly machine to turn four furrows at a time?

Unfortunately the whole business of cultivation today is about time and logistics. The stubble must be turned the day after it was shorne so that it can be sown, or oil-seed rape put down to change the colour of the carpeted landscape. What has been lost is skill and man's close contact with the earth from which he derives his very existence. Gray's ploughman has, once and for all, wended homeward his weary way. His long walk is over. It can't be said that the ploughman's world was ever entirely idyllic. His landship, as the horse-plough was sometimes called, cut a furrow through cowslips and yarrow, vetch and thistle, leaving behind it a smooth, evenly ironed furrow over which yelping gulls sailed or glided. With the passing of months the whole surface of the former pasture became a wonderful pattern of straight furrows boxed by a ploughed headland on which, in due time, peewits might nest and mad March hares sport themselves.

When it was all done, the ploughman skidded his plough to the implement shed and brought out the harrows and the roller. Summer came, with hay-making before corn harvest, and there he was, back again, ploughing out the potato crop with the ridger or hiller, and actually looking forward to the long walk once again with the occasional ploughing match to brighten the darker days of November. Without his labour the sower, who walked the furrows broadcasting corn by the handful, or scattering it with a device called a 'fiddle', would have nothing to do, nor would he himself be there to gather peewits' eggs in spring, sending them to hotels in the big cities to provide a very special treat for their wealthier patrons. They might not have been all jolly fellows who followed the plough, but they took great pride in their work and loved their horses, grooming and feeding them at the end of every day – always before they even thought of going for their own supper. It is sad that the painted-up plough on the pub forecourt tells nothing of this.

The Plough

ARTRIDGES ARE never very conspicuous birds; for, although they occasionally roost in the thorn trees of a low-growing, thick hedge in winter, they are ground birds in the true sense. Hatched in the long grass or in the bramble bush on the hedge bank, they have the ability to get up and go soon afterwards. Never needing to be fed by their parent, they escape the attention of predators like the brown rat who, having found a feast of eggs, returns to the nest again and again until he has taken them all.

When the partridge's clutch of eggs has escaped the attention of the rat, or the watchful magpie or crow, the hatched brood moves quietly away into the jungle of the long grass. Here, if they are disturbed, they will immediately scatter in all directions, working their way into the cover round about and resting there motionless until the predator has gone. The hen decides when it is safe to move and, with an almost inaudible cheeping, reassures her frightened brood and gathers them together so that they can move on. They learn from her where to find the grubs and insects and the places where the seeds they like best are to be found. They travel down the rows of the turnip field, the furrows of the potato planting, and through the green, leafy tunnels of the kale field and, at mid-day, when the sun is warm, they gather on the bare patch, some knoll where they can sunbathe and have a dustbath. When fully fledged, in company with their parent, they sail over the hedge and whirr away, a covey that will stay together through the winter and only break up at the coming of spring.

The little brown birds of the furrows, as they have been called, have always been hunted. Man used to net the partridge covey by walking the field in which it settled to roost for the night and dropping his net over them. The gun enabled him with the aid of setters or pointing dogs to shoot the covey, one by one, as it flew on to settle and be discovered again by its relentless pursuers. The game laws protected the partridge from the poacher and left it to the mercy of the landowner. Some landowners loved partridge shooting so much that their keepers were instructed to gather the eggs, bring them on under a broody hen, and take them back to hatch naturally under the bird that had laid them. This was achieved by leaving the wild partridge dummy eggs to sit on while her own eggs were protected both from predators and the cold rain in a bad summer. Partridges decline in numbers in bad years and landowners lament that the native bird (the red-legged partridge seen in the southern counties is also known as a Frenchman) is dying out in some places.

Partridges

N DAYS GONE BY, when, apart from those Roman roads Britain had inherited from the Caesars, communications between county towns and market towns and villages beyond were poor indeed, farmers who grew wheat, barley or oats needed to have their grain harvest milled to provide themselves with flour and oatmeal. The mill had to be within reasonable distance from the farm, about as far as a team could haul a wagon there and back again. The journey to the mill would be painful and demanding when the terrain was hilly. A team could do much more on the flat countryside of East Anglia, for instance, than it could in the dales of Derbyshire, where millstone grit provided material essential to the production of stone-ground flour. Windmills atop hills turned merrily enough, but where there were hills there were valleys and in the depths of the dales water-powered flour mills were to be found.

The economy of the arable farmer made it essential that he got his grain harvest through the mill and onto the market as quickly as possible. Cities depended on the corn grown in their immediate vicinity and the miller was an important cog in the wheel. Flour went to local bakeries. If man didn't live by bread alone it was still the staff of life, and many poor people had little else on which to keep body and soul together. No one had yet needed to say that bread should really contain the wheatgerm – that nothing should be taken out to be sold back to the customer as breakfast cereal or dog biscuit. Year in, year out, the jolly miller kept the grindstone grinding. The village baker baked his bread. In farmhouses in places where no wheat was grown, sacks of flour were kept in bunkers to make what today is still called farmhouse bread, the flour was once traded for oats at the local mill, and the remainder of the oat crop fed to horses, pigs and fowl. This was part of a closely integrated economy in which flour milling was particularly important.

The jolly miller was not always such a jolly fellow. For him an occupational hazard was a disease like farmer's lung. Before he reached retirement it was almost certain he would go down with a respiratory complaint for which there was no cure. The many hundreds of flour mills that once dotted the length and breadth of Britain are reduced to a few, most of which are curiosities and not working mills in the old sense of the word. Milling has been centralised. Derelict waterwheels are to be found in waterless sluices. Skeleton sail mills, most with their timbers rotting, are renovated and restored from time to time to make tourist attractions. Harvested grain now goes from silos to the milling centre. The day of the working windmill and watermill is over.

The Journey to the Mill

HEN WILLIAM COBBETT surveyed the counties of England and gave an account in his celebrated *Rural Rides*, he deplored the decline in the numbers of congregations at country churches. In the early decades of the nineteenth century the rural population was in decline. Churches were showing signs of neglect. Parsons with livings in the gift of the squire were too often absent from their parishes, hunting, or worse, hob-nobbing with their wealthier patrons at spas and popular resorts. It wasn't the fault of the parson, or any lack of zeal on his part, that brought about the sad situation where a congregation of three sat listening to his sermon on a bleak winter's day. The rural population had filtered away as men found jobs created by the industrial revolution.

Country folk had been, in the main, God-fearing and devoted to their church, although often the squire insisted upon there being no backsliders among his employees and tenants. As ever, the country church remains in many places the focal point for worship or for the social contact attendance at church promotes. The parson co-ordinates the activities of groups of women who devote their time to decorating the church with flowers, doing social work of one sort or another, or engaging themselves in sewing, handicrafts, cookery and so on. With a congregation spread more thinly on the ground than that of his counterpart in the market town, the rector knows not only the faces of his flock, but their most intimate affairs.

Come harvest festival the women bring flowers, generally the flowers of their own cottage gardens, and vie with one another decorating the church from porch to altar. Their menfolk fork the vegetable garden to dig up and carefully select their finest potatoes, carrots, parsnips or beetroot, all of them presented with as much care as for the annual flower and vegetable show. Vegetable marrows lie beside jars of home-made jam because the combine dispenses nothing but tangles of straw and showers of grain. Where the art of making a corn dolly still survives, there will be beautifully plaited stalks of wheat, intricate work executed by someone to whom this art has been handed down by father or grandfather. Harvest home is not, of course, the only time the ladies of the congregation get together to decorate the church. The porch has hardly been tidied up and the aisles swept before they are back at work decorating it over again for Christmas and helping to build that minor work of art, the thatched manger with the holy infant nestled in hay. The wonderful thing is that these customs are as old as the churches themselves.

The Country Church

HE DITCH THAT runs along the boundary of the hedge bank is as important to the condition of the pasture as it is to the health and productivity of the cultivated field. Into this open drain that farther down feeds the stream, which in turn is the feeder of the river, run the land drains of red clay tiles or more ancient draining systems of stone, rubble or even brushwood. In some cases the ditches are fed by natural springs of pure water filtered by gravel or sand as they cross the bedrock.

The ditch has a life of its own. It may serve as a watering hole for cattle. It may shelter waterbirds like the wagtail and the water hen that find nesting places along its course. The yellowhammer may nest on the hedge bank above with the hedgesparrow, and the ditch, where it broadens, provide a minor pool or pond where a pair of wintering teal will swim, and mallards paddle to dip for weed. Ditches or fen drains, as those long sedgey cuttings across East Anglia are called, may also support fish, the loach and the eel, which the old grey heron will hunt. Frogs and toads emerge from the weeds and freshwater shrimps live in a swaying forest of cress and duckweed.

The ditch and the feeder are only spoilt when there is pollution; a seepage of fertiliser that concentrates when the water of the stream is low. Here and there a farmer without conscience lets his pig slurry run into the open drain and kills everything for a mile or more below his piggery. As time goes by the ditch slowly fills with decaying vegetable matter and dead wood. It had to be cleaned out and the traditional way was for the ditcher to come along with his long-handled shovel and scoop out everything, the silt, the gravel, the clumps of weed and the lumps of wood, throwing it all onto the bank. The poor frog loses his shelter. The eel, thrown out into the grass unerringly wriggles his way back to the water and swims upstream, avoiding the ditcher's feet and finding what cover he can in the gravelly stream-bed higher up.

The ditcher's work was seasonal and generally done between harvests, never in 'February fill-dyke' when there is always a flood or spate, but when it was important to improve the drainage of an arable field to be put under the plough again or bear the weight of cornbinder or wagons. The old time ditcher's modern counterpart, like the hedger's, is a relentless mechanical monster. Time is money, and no farmer wants to pay a man for weeks doing what a machine can do in a day. The ditcher may have loved his work and enjoyed shovelling out the eel or getting himself a few crayfish for supper, but the crayfish have long since been poisoned and he himself is redundant.

The Ditcher

EDGES MAY BE disappearing from the rural landscape at the rate of several thousand miles a year. Thousands of miles of ancient hedge have certainly been grubbed up, for one reason or another, since the present century began. It is a sad thought that man can no more make a hedge than he can make a tree, without waiting for the hedge to grow. None of the so-called quicksets provides a barrier to livestock that the farmer needs. There is nothing like the green thorn tree, the briar, and the tough old blackthorn, for discouraging animals from breaking out of their field. Hedges require that much more attention than drystone walls, for the thorn will grow higher and leave gaps; a ewe will push her way through. The pig that wanders puts his snout into the brambles and forces his way out, and there is always one such animal in the herd to lead the rest in search of greener grass elsewhere.

The hedger's trade was often linked to the ditcher's, both having their seasons. His tools were the hedgeknife and the billhook. Armed with these he would make his way steadily from one corner of the field to the next, slashing the briar and topping the thorn so that it would grow bushier, sparing the ash sapling and the young field maple to grow into hedge trees in due time. Here and there he would be forced to do a stretch of fencing, hopefully leaving the young thorns to weave themselves into a permanent barrier and keep out a neighbour's ill-provided-for sheep or horses. Time makes a hedge and, while the hedge may draw nourishment from the headland as its roots spread farther into the field, it also provides shelter for the wintering flock and beasts that would otherwise starve in the east wind. Even the arable field derives some benefit from the windbreak.

Time and circumstances have combined to force farmers to mechanise even hedge-trimming. Local authorities, also, have had to look at their costs. The townsman who sails out to enjoy the countryside and admires beech hedges, hedges of yew and layered hedges may wonder in passing why some farmers and estate owners are so neglectful of their boundaries, forgetting that even the small hedge round his suburban garden costs money to keep. Hedge-laying is a skill that is now rare. There is no better barrier, but it can't be done to every hedge, except by a millionaire. It is one of the rural crafts that is also an art, but, sadly, one practised by fewer and fewer men as the years pass.

The Hedger

OTTAGE GARDENS are never entirely beds of roses with lavender bushes and pink-flowering currants sheltering fluffed-up bantams, though there are many lovely cottages that stand in idyllic surroundings. There is a world of difference between the pretty cottage garden and the cottager's garden, for the former is there as an expression of creativity and the latter is part of the country dwellers' economy, and is necessary to his livelihood.

The garden may have its lavender and thyme, its gilly flowers, hollyhocks and delphiniums. Tea rose and honeysuckle may drench the evening air with their perfume while turtle doves purr, but behind the ancient dwelling lies the vegetable garden with perhaps an old apple or an old pear tree that still bears a fair crop in a good season. Here the soil has been continually enriched and improved until it might be dug with bare hands, so deep and good is its tilth. Hundredweights of manure and humus of different origins have gone into it to produce an unbelievable yield of King Edwards or Arran Pilot. No finer carrots are grown by any professional. Parsnips there are to lie on the cottager's plate and make his mouth water, and there are beetroots, onions and shallots. The rhubarb patch is for jam-making. Fat marrows break from their covering of long-stemmed leaves and, if there are weeds – chickweed and groundsel for the birds – it is only because the cottager hasn't enough hours in his day to do everything that needs to be done in his garden. He must find time in spring to 'get the garden in', a task that is almost a ritual as he opens a row and fills it with manure to grow his potatoes, and then he must get his peas in and make sure they are properly protected from the birds. He looks at his bean poles and renews them with hazel cut from the hedge or the copse. He sets a tip-up trap for the rat that runs the row, or even for the mole that burrows his way, regardless of the potato planting or the newly sown lettuce and cabbage. His bees pollinate the apple tree and ensure that his raspberry bushes will bear a good crop. His wife will be glad of both crops, one for her apple pies and the other for jam.

Labour in his garden is a labour of love and he forgets the backache, working for himself, making his own potato clamp, bringing in his own harvest of carrots and storing them against the frost. In harder times the garden was often all that stood between the family and penury, but even in the day of packaged food and the deep freeze nothing the cottager eats can taste half as good as the things he grows and harvests by the sweat of his brow. No piece of ground means more to him.

The Cottage Garden

HATCH IS WITHOUT doubt one of the oldest ways employed by man to keep a dry roof over his head. The material was always plentiful, even before wheat was extensively cultivated, for the marshlands provided long-stemmed reeds, which, the more they were cut, grew taller and more suitable for the purpose. Reeds will often grow to a towering eight feet. Wheat straw, the alternative material, will barely grow to half that length, but both, in the hands of the skilled thatcher, can provide a roof covering that will last a generation before serious damage occurs.

Devon thatch is straw thatch. Norfolk is reed, because reeds were always the natural crop of the fens and, in addition to cottages and barns, fenland churches were often thatched. With luck a well-thatched roof might last for even seventy years. In this time the sedge ridge-covering will have been renewed regularly and sections of the eighteen inches' thick, double layer of reed or wheat straw, showing signs of letting water in, will have been redone by the skilled thatcher. The most vulnerable part of the 'butted' reed or straw is the end of the material, the place where it may not only rot, but be attacked by the pests that plague the life of anyone living under an old thatch. Birds remorselessly pull out straws and strive to make a hole so that they can nest in the attic or build an equally snug nest in the cavity they have made. Rats may follow in due course and, once a thatched roof begins to slump, there is no remedy but to get the thatcher back on the job.

A first-class thatch is usually fastened to the rafters by means of hooks, driven in to hold down the reed after the thatcher has located the position of the support by probing. The process of laying on begins at the eaves and is carried upwards, layer after layer held down by hazel rods, and each bundle of thatch is thoroughly beaten to ensure an even butt. Rain must run down the butt from ridge to eaves without seeping into the covering as a whole. The reed thatcher works atop the roof, but there is another method employed by some straw thatchers who use twine, threaded through to hold the covering when a man, working from the inside, pushes the needle back to a companion on the outside, enabling him to pull everything tight to the rafter. A much less durable thatch is employed in some places where straw is simply 'laid' on the rafters, but it has to be kept secure with netting to prevent the birds taking the covering away, straw by straw. Insurance may be expensive and frequent maintenance necessary, but there is much to be said for living in fairyland and waking to the twittering of birds immediately above one's bed.

Thatching

INCE THE FIRST FIELD was delineated, and man found it necessary to keep things in while keeping others out, he has been a waller, builder of pens and sheepfolds from boulders near to hand, quarrying local stone to enclose more and more ground from the bottom of the valley away up to the highest skyline. Some walls are of great antiquity, while others are the result of more recent land enclosure acts, but where there was stone, man used it.

He needed to conserve timber sometimes for other purposes. Hedges took too long to grow, and when he cultivated a field he often ploughed out more stones than he knew what to do with. He would use these stones to reinforce his old walls or sometimes build them into new walls with clods of earth, a fashion regularly employed in Devon. Cotswold stone is famous and there is nothing more handsome than a perfectly built wall of Cotswold stone. Like limestone, Cotswold quarried stone lends itself to regular construction. A template is employed to make sure the contour is maintained on any particular stretch of wall being put up, the completed wall may then be topped with coping stones. In limestone and mortar walls encountered in parts of North Wales, the containing stonework is filled in with limestone rubble, broken limestone or quarry residue particularly suitable as a core. The coping stones, solidly mortared in place, discourage the most agile sheep or goat from climbing out of, or into the ground enclosed. The only danger to the solid structure that may finally bring it tumbling down is when humus accumulates between the coping stones and seeds germinate. Plants like valerian or elder, taking root, force their way down and dislodge the coping. When this happens, and the roots find more room, they may burst the wall and the rubble within spills out.

It is even more difficult to find a man with the waller's skills for it is one of those crafts that is fast dying. There are no apprentices. Few can afford to build in stone. It is fascinating to think of the price a present-day landowner would have to pay for walls built to enclose grazing, either drystone-walled or mortar-walled. The 'dike' in Scotland is a traditional drystone wall that contains both pasture and arable land. Being entirely constructed without consolidating material, it needs regular attention, for cattle are capable of bringing a wall down by rubbing against it. Here, the farmer has to acquire a little of the dike-builder's skill when he sets about rebuilding above an avalanche created by an escaping flock of black-faced sheep. The craft is revived and encouraged by drystone walling competitions, but very few of the entrants earn their living building new drystone walls.

Walling

HERE BUT in the country would there be room for the old orchard? The professional orchardsman may have a forest of healthy young trees bearing the maximum crop of James Grieve or Cox's, completely unblemished, because, not only has his well-ordered plantation been fertilised, but his trees carefully pruned, banded and sprayed at exactly the right time in the season. Alas, the average countryman watches his precious tree grow old and gnarled, like his old grandfather, but looks upon it with affection when it blossoms once again, and every five or six years has a crop to make up for the years between when it gave him only a hatful of apples to stew with a handful of blackberries and make into a pie.

The old tree shades a corner of the garden. In twisted and interlocking branches that should have been cut out with a pruning saw, a mistlethrush or a collared dove builds a nest. The summer cuckoo pauses to settle briefly and tell the world that it has arrived at last, its call echoing in the nearby beech wood. When the old tree bears its crop in a year of plenty, so does the cross-pollinator close by, as well as the tree beyond that, planted even earlier by the cottager who loved apple trees, but never thought about his capacity to eat apple pie or apple dumpling. A hundred apples fall to the grass. A few remain high, far beyond the reach of the pickers. The greedy jay will alight on a slender branchlet and feast on sun-ripened fruit, striking the apple again and again until it finally falls to the ground. It rolls into the long grass providing a feast for the field mouse and the spring-heeled squirrel that bounces his way along from the bottom of one tree to the next in search of another apple, a Russet or Prince Albert.

Most of the old orchard trees have lost their names. A few may be identified by old men who remember the taste of a once highly thought-of variety. One or two go into decline without ever being identified except as the apple 'old missis so-and-so' made her apple jelly from, an apple of such wonderful colour and flavour that no one can imagine how such trees went out of fashion. Old trees are grubbed out and new ones planted in their place occasionally, but a young orchard will never pay for itself unless managed by an expert. The old trees are spared because they are pleasant to look at in apple blossom time. Occasionally the countryman who knows very little about root pruning or ring-barking will load his shotgun and shoot the old tree that hasn't had an apple on it for years. Sometimes a miracle results and the tree bears fruit, the shotgun wound doing exactly what ring-barking would have done.

Apple Picking

 HUNDRED YEARS before anyone dreamt of a butter mountain or a milk goat, almost every small farmer kept two or three cows which provided the family with milk and butter, with a little over to be offered in midsummer at market when grass was plentiful and the cow was giving of her best. Butter and eggs, nearly always matching one another in price, the same few pence for a dozen fresh eggs as for a pound of salty, farm butter, were needed to supplement the family income. Every week or so that farmer's wife, having carefully skimmed cream from her few gallons of milk each day, would scald the cream and the churn to set about her butter-making in the time honoured fashion.

A variety of churns may be seen in old farm museums: a dasher churn, which might have been inspired by a washtub dolly, and barrel churns that were so much easier to use. Both barrel churns were rotated by a crank, one rotating vertically and the other horizontally, and both having a milk-tight, or cream-tight, lid. Cream turns to butter when the fat content of the milk separates from the rest. The end products are butter and buttermilk, and the process is not unlike cheese-making which results in separating curd from whey. Turning the churn at an even speed eventually brings about the golden nuggets of butter in thinned buttermilk. The operator watches for this in a little glass window that at first carries a film of milk and then gradually clears to become speckled soon afterwards with tiny flecks of butter. When the window is clear again and the butter nuggets are beginning to amalgamate, the lid of the churn is unscrewed and the buttermilk strained off through a muslin cloth. The process is yet far from completion for the churned butter has to be beaten until all liquid, butter-milk and water, has been forced out. Finally, the carefully measured and weighed pats of butter are wrapped for market, some of them decorated by means of a mould leaving the imprint of perhaps a rose, a thistle, or a sheaf of wheat.

All this, and the skill of the dairymaid, has disappeared from the scene in fifty or sixty years. The factory began to take over when the first vegetable oil product called margarine began to appear on the market. Dairy farmers scornfully dubbed it refined axle grease and doubted its future, little thinking that in a short time the focus of the dairy industry would be in vast plants designed to take the labour out of butter churning, and, some people still insist, the real taste out of country butter!

The Butterchurn

HERE IS HARDLY a country parish in rural Britain without a lake, pond, stream, meandering or turbulent river in which fish of one aspect or another are found. Some of the brooding ponds in remote places contain carp, bream or pike and perch, fish that are thought little of by the cook in modern times. The carp is a classic example of the stew-pond fish brought to this country so that the monastery could have its fish on Friday; but, when communications were so poor, any kind of fish, muddy-tasting or not, was welcomed on the labourer's table. If his master fished for the lordly salmon and reserved the fishing on the chalk stream for himself, because the brown trout was much more to his liking than what are known as coarse fish, the peasant went forth with a makeshift rod and perhaps no reel, or 'wheel', at all with which to play his pike or perch. The garden worm or the entrails of a fowl were good enough bait and necessity forbade any pre-occupation with what might have been considered sporty and what was not. In the sixteenth century few of the fishermen who sought sport on either the great salmon rivers of the north or the idyllic reaches of Itchen, Test or Kennet thought of finer fishing rods and the design of the reel. Such things took their time. Great brown trout swam in the mill pools or had their moorings in green jungles of waterweed through which pure rivers flowed. God was in the fisherman's heaven. The bittern boomed in the reeds, and kingfishers fished while the colley bird, the white-bibbed dipper, walked into the torrent and the very heart of the flood to get food for its nestlings under the bridge.

Who owns a fish that lives naturally and by chance where it is found swimming in a pond or river? Great tomes of law have been compiled to answer this seemingly simple question. The river belongs to the man whose land it crosses and what lives in it is his, although the countryman has always had an obstinate mind and has often gone to prison before being convinced that he must accept this law. However, the fishing fraternity now regulates itself so that, with few exceptions, most manage to fish where they can pay their way. Large fishing clubs rent stretches of water in the heart of the country and their members come to fish ancient ponds and stews first stocked in Norman times. Fly-fishers ply their carbon-fibre rods in put-and-take fisheries and all have their sport where once only the privileged landowner might fish.

Fishing

VEN IN THE FAR-OFF days when an ordinary man who put up a gun to shoot a pheasant risked transportation to the Antipodes without a return ticket available to him after he had served his seven years, wildfowling tended to be in a class of its own. The great landowner might lay claim to the riverbank, the estuary and even the shore, but below high-water mark the commoner might get himself a wintering wigeon or a goose. In the wilderness of East Anglian marshes, as near jungle as could be found in the British Isles, the old professional fowlers plied their trade and cultivated skills that enabled them to make great bags of different sorts of fowl that were readily bought by London merchants.

Duck were lured into tunnel decoys, and rafts of wigeon, that floated on the swell of the rising tide while waiting for dusk and their nocturnal feeding along the banks of the river, were stalked by fowlers with skiffs armed with enormous scatterguns capable of killing scores of birds at a single shot. The snare of the fowler got him other birds such as woodcock and snipe. He knew how to rig nets as well as how to set wires. He studied the flight lines of his quarry and got to know where the geese would go when the wind was in a particular direction. This trade was seasonal, of course, because it depended upon the north–south migration of certain species. Geese came in from Greenland and Iceland, from Scandinavia and the ice wastes of Russia. Ducks came in thousands to shelter in the long lanes of reeds and the minor lakes and bays of lowland waterways in the Broads. It wasn't that the landowner didn't appreciate the natural bounty that he might have claimed as exclusively his. Wildfowling always had a degree of hardship, acute suffering at times, for the man stalking his prey among frozen reeds and through icy pools. A goose is often tough and not always edible and duck may taste as much of mud as the fish that comes out of the same stagnant water. Woodcock are to be had in pheasant coverts in mid-winter, and are far easier to get than fowl in the marsh.

Wildfowl, it was agreed, almost without saying, were fair enough game for the 'shore-popper' and the marsh creeper who paddled his skiff into the mist and lined up his cannon of a fowling piece, his very breath freezing in his beard as he did so. The punt gun has now gone to the museum. The present-day fowler may arm himself with a repeating shotgun but must content himself with a much smaller bag.

Wildfowling

HE BEST CIDER comes from those parts of southern Britain where cider apples have always been grown: Devon, Somerset, Gloucester, Hereford, Worcester and, to a lesser degree, the counties of Kent and Norfolk. The favourite varieties of cider apple are as time-honoured as the favourite cooking and dessert apples the British housewife has always bought, but their names are more colourful and rustic – Kingston Black, Cheatboy, Foxwhelp, Bloody Butcher, Yarlington Mill, and Cap of Liberty.

Although cider is sold commercially, both in bottles and as draught, and is available as sweet and dry under a variety of brand names, the traditional west country product was mainly brewed for home consumption and known as rough or scrumpy. This may still be bought in a west country pub straight from the barrel, and many an innocent holidaymaker has succumbed to its quite disconcerting delayed-action effect. It depends, as all good brews do, on the original sugar content of the ingredients, but it can be as potent as strong ale, and leave the man who takes too many glasses of the stuff with a nasty headache the following day. The apple harvest is a 'back-end' event and it makes little difference to the final product whether the apples fallen into the orchard grass were bruised or turned brown.

Their destination is the cider mill, generally a piece of ancient equipment that may be hand-operated, or powered by a sturdy workhorse on a 'walk' mill. Whether the apples are crushed by more sophisticated means, or put through the old mangle, the object is to produce pomace from which the apple juice will be pressed, strained, and finally siphoned off to be fermented, a process that may take a week or ten days. Straining in the first instance may be through hessian. In some cases straw is also used, although straw can give an unwanted flavour to the end product. Even the pressed-out juice will be nothing like that crystal-clear, commercially produced glass of branded cider and, when it goes into the casks, casks that once held wine or spirit, where the final ferment takes place, impurities will surge in the cloth-stopper bung-hole. These will be cleared and the barrel re-stoppered in the same way after the vessel has been topped up. This topping up is essential to the production of drinkable rough or sweet cider, or vinegar will result. Rough cider was almost everywhere the west country farmer's substitute for home-brewed beer. It was cheaper to make when he had a good orchard by his door. Hodge always had a thirst and his master would take care to see that he made enough rough for both his family and the work force. The residue of pulp might be fed to cattle. Pigs would take the sludge.

Cider-making

I F AN ENGLISHMAN'S HOME is his castle, beer is his favourite drink whether he drinks it from a straight glass or the pewter pot. So far as he is concerned there is no drink quite like it. What has saddened the dedicated beer drinker most in recent years is an intervention of the chemist between himself and the master brewer, the man who put the hops in his pint and produced good bitter beer. What the chemist had to do, when he produced something that looked like a clear pint of ale, was gas it up to put a head on the stuff. It had to be beer if it looked like beer, and the thirsty customer would hardly know the difference once the first pint had gone down. Alas for the chemist, the rude forefathers of the village were not all gone to their long rest. Some had sat on the very same settle when the landlord himself had served them with a pint of best, brewed on the premises! It had cost tuppence a pint. It had been real strong stuff. Young lads had fallen about groping for the sneck of the door when they had had no more than two pints of it. What the marketing experts overlooked was nostalgia. Beer had always been cheaper, stronger, and had more body in it. It had real hops in it. Everyone knew that chemists were imitating the flavour of the hop. How long was it since anyone had found a hop in his pintpot? Once upon a time, the old ones muttered, whole families had gone off to Kent for the hop-picking. Now most of the pickers were redundant. The call for hops was no more. This wasn't true of course. The big breweries did all they could to persuade the drinker that he didn't really know what was good for him.

'Real' ale was a device the small brewer employed to steal a share of the market. A good pint was a well-kept pint. The stainless steel barrel was much more hygienic than the old wooden one. A hop in the glass said something about the way beer was produced in hole-in-the-corner, old-fashioned breweries that would no longer pass inspection. Area managers tried to contradict the heresy that their beer was a chemical product boosted with carbon dioxide, but the sheer obstinacy of the beer drinker, who always studied his pint before he swallowed it, prevailed. Even the big brewers had to acknowledge that the customer wasn't always wrong. Real ale was advertised as one of the brews available in pubs that cared for their customers and would be on tap, without gas, anything put in, or anything taken out. Simultaneously a new campaign attempted to persuade the undiscriminating drinker to ask for lager. One day there may be no hop poles or hop-pickers on the Kentish landscape, but will good English beer ever be forgotten?

The Hopfield

HILE THE WORKING horse powered most agricultural implements and pulled the wagon and the brewer's dray, blacksmiths were to be found in almost every rural parish. Not all of them worked in an idyllic world of ringing anvils and flying sparks. The romantic image of the blacksmith as a powerful, heavily muscled man was more fiction than fact. He was more likely to be a wiry individual with great stamina, who worked long hours and was always dehydrated by the heat of the forge. He was at the beck and call of the farmers who waited impatiently for their teams to be shod or who had implements that needed continual re-fettling.

There were some smiths, a few who were not much more than show-smiths, farriers, others with intimate knowledge of the anatomy and the ailments of the heavy horse. Some of these 'horse doctors' knew as much as the vet and were consulted by the farming community to avoid the vet's fees. In general, smiths followed in the footsteps of their fathers and grandfathers from whom they inherited secrets of the trade, remedies for the sicknesses of horses and ponies, and ways of working, hardening and tempering metal. When a horse walked badly and was to be sold the smith could fit it with a shoe that would disguise the fault. He could also make sets of shoes that would keep an animal on its feet when the hills were glazed with ice and loads of grain or milkchurns had to be transported to the mill or the creamery.

Here and there the smith was more than a tradesman, and could fashion ornamental gates or make special ploughs for ploughing competitions. The really skilled smith could hand-weld and lay out a carpet of links to make chain harrows, forming the links one by one on the toe of the anvil. When he had teams to shoe the smith would snub one of the pair to a ring in the wall, leaving the second horse tethered outside, quickly take the old shoes off the animal he was to work on, and pare the hooves after making sure he had pulled out the old nails. In some cases two complete sets of shoes would be kept ready for the team and getting the animals re-shod would take only a short time, but even the 'ready-mades' would have to go back into the fire and each shoe applied hot to the animal's hoof. There is no more acrid smell than that of burning hoof or horn, but the shoeing smith was well used to it.

When the working horse began to disappear some blacksmiths became mechanics and bought themselves welding outfits and compressors to provide an air blast when they used a forge, while others quickly advertised themselves as available for 'cold shoeing' and took their work out to pony stables.

A Blacksmith

O ONE CAN SAY for certain when and how the hybrid, common gamebird that is only here and there a truly wild bird, and generally a pampered creature looked after by keepers, came from the far east in the first place. Its name has a Phoenician ring to it but its origin must have been in Burma or Malaysia. It thrives in Britain, particularly in more southerly parts of the country. The privilege of shooting it once depended on ownership of land, until a long succession of laws defining what game is, and what trespass in its pursuit amounts to finally brought a challenge allowing the ordinary man to shoot the pheasant if he had a licence and access to land on which the bird might be found. Keepering is really a business of shepherding young pheasants and partridges on land where they have been established, reared and provided with the necessary cover and food. Always when the farm labourer, or the farmer himself, sought to shoot or snare a bird that wandered close to his door, the law was invoked and the offender, if a mere labourer, could find himself transported. The farmer would be put off his farm. If he owned the farm it had to be large enough to entitle him to the privilege of shooting game. No smallholder had this right, but in the bad old days even the great landowner was hard to put to it to fill his larder with pheasants. He lacked the kind of gun that would enable him to shoot more than one at a time. His weapon would be muzzle-loading, a flintlock perhaps, prone to the flash in the pan or letting the powder become damp. One at a time was 'good fishing', and this was all the sporting squire could hope for.

It wasn't until the nineteenth century that the *battue* was made possible by the invention of the breech-loading, double-barrelled shotgun. This weapon derived from the muzzle-loader fired by means of a percussion cap, an improvement that overcame the many drawbacks of the old flintlock. The breech-loading shotgun was further improved and the shooting gentleman began to stand at the side of the wood and have birds driven over him. This system was used everywhere to improve 'sport'. The pheasant was reared in ever-increasing numbers until bags of several hundreds were made by the great shots of the day using beautifully balanced ejectors that sometimes got almost too hot to handle. No one can say why such enormous bags of pheasants are killed. The bird costs a great deal more to rear and raise than the gamedealer or his customer could afford to pay for it, but of course the cultivated pheasant isn't the only animal that is bred and slaughtered. Field sports, like stock farming and shepherding, are about killing.

Pheasant Shooting

T HE WORLD OF JOHN PEEL and the cry of his hounds in the morning was a much wilder one than that of Mr Jorrocks but a spectacle country folk have always enjoyed wherever there is a meet. It may be argued that hunting makes very little impression on the fox population of the shires, hunted by traditional country packs with famous names – Belvoir, Quorn and Cottesmore – but, of course, hunting is not really about killing foxes. It is a social occasion, an exercise for hounds, the enjoyment of a special atmosphere that surrounds the meet with hounds weaving through one another, the huntsman and the whipper-in keeping an anxious eye on everything, and the Master acknowledging subscribers and their guests, some in immaculate habits, and some less well kitted out but no less enthusiastic. The earth-stopper has made a tour of all the earths in his parish. The fox, lying out somewhere in a gorse clump or in a forest of dead bracken, knows that something is afoot. He is hardly a cub. He has the most sensitive ears and he knows every bit of cover, every avenue of escape from the place in which he had been lying. The Master of the Hunt, with the advice of the huntsman and perhaps the keeper, as well as other estate servants, has already decided which cover will be drawn first. If no fox is found the pack will be rallied and bustle onto the next. Cantering together, subscribers will exchange pleasantries and gossip, and perhaps arrive late to find the pack yelping and swarming over hillocks and through scrub because they have a faint, still lingering scent of Old Charlie. After a while a gate will be opened and the field will trot along the woodside, the heels of their mounts throwing up lumps of mud and small clods of grass while the wood echoes with the voices of hunt servants, 'Did you see him?' someone may ask; 'He gave us the slip! I saw him go over the hill just as we were closing the gate!' But imagination plays tricks. The huntsman blows his horn and the field is suddenly roused and moves from a jog to a positive canter and finally to a gallop. The old fox in the bracken slips off while the field pursues another that threads his way across country, his scent exciting hounds, but drifting, far off track.

This is what everyone came for, the fences, the ditches, the hard ride. A hunted fox doesn't turn back and takes another line if needs be. Often only the huntsman sees the fox and the Master canters wearily home at the end of it all forgetting that he set out with a conviction that this was to be a red-letter day. Fox-hunting is certainly not an efficient way of killing a fox. More foxes die of old age.

The Hunt

HE WILD GOOSE in flight over the winter fields is a sight that stirs most people, for most of the wintering geese have come down from arctic regions to enjoy a milder climate than they would in the tundra. Indeed, if the greylay or pinkfoot remained in the wilderness it would die. The lichens and other items of food it enjoys in the short summer of long daylight are buried in snow and sheated in ice. Something tells the geese it is time to go, and they come down out of the north, from Greenland, Iceland, Spitzbergen and Russia. They settle in the milder climate of the Fens, and other parts of Britain where they find food on corn stubbles, old potato fields, fields of frosted carrots, pastures on which they will browse like flocks of sheep.

They are a romantic sight to most people, welcome enough on the stubbles, not begrudged the small potatoes they unearth on the potato field, but unwanted on the pasture. Ten geese may eat as much as a single sheep, depriving the sheep of nourishment, and driving the shepherd to despair for he is compelled to make up the deficiency with expensive feedstuffs, but the farmer has little time to stalk them when they settle. He knows how wary they are even when they are down on his vegetable field. The flock has a roster of sentinel geese that keep their heads high and warn the rest when danger is imminent. A man with the gun, stalking the flock on the edge of a reedy drain, knows that if he doesn't keep down the flock will be in the air, sailing away, yelping their complaint, conversing with one another while a new field is looked for.

The omnivorous character of most of the goose family makes them as much at home on grass as on the tundra. They dibble and dabble to unearth the frosted carrot on the deserted vegetable field, and, when they have had their fill, rise in a trailing mass to find a roosting place far enough out on the open water or the exposed sands to keep them safe from harm until the following day. They move as though they had a built-in, synchronised clock at the same time every morning and the same hour in the afternoon. They arrive in their wintering area on almost the same day each autumn, and depart in the same month each spring. If man wanted reassurance on the continuity of life and things unchanged, it is in the habit of geese that come and go, year after year, as they have done since the ice age.

Wild Geese

HERE WAS A TIME when the great landowners, more concerned with rearing pheasants and partridges than the welfare of their tenant farmers, forbade the harvesting of corn on their estates except with a sickle. A delayed harvest might mean that the tenant would find it difficult to get the rent together, and be thrown off the estate on that account, but it allowed ground birds to enjoy the grain and survive in fields of wheat or oats until the shooting season was properly under way. Things had to change of course, for Britain depended upon agriculture for its survival and its stability.

Soon the sickle and the scythe were put aside to make room for a corn reaper, a horse-drawn implement that left the wheat or oats in swaths to be lifted and tied by harvesters following behind. This gave place to a much cleverer invention, the cornbinder. Now with this flailing machine, with a built-in conveyor belt to feed the shorn stalks squarely into its involved sequence of sheaf-making cams and levers, the workers who followed no longer needed to lift and tie sheaves. All they had to do was stook, or build the sheaves head-to-head in groups of four along the path the machine had cut. Harvest was suddenly speeded up. The backache had been taken out of it all, even if more horses were needed to pull the cornbinder – three, where two had been used, and occasionally even five to cut corn on the very steep hill. What harvest had always been about was getting corn built into ricks before it was wasted by the weather and began to grow in the sheaf, sprouting green again while the straw began to rot. The cornbinder had so many working parts and received such a hammering in the process of cutting corn that the local blacksmith was continually called out when the contraption began to show signs of wear. Everyone knew that it would one day have to be consigned to the scrap heap, and its days were numbered when the horses were put to grass and the old machine was hitched behind the tractor. When things reached this stage someone looked at the threshing machine and decided that the answer lay in nailing two great lumps of machinery together, and the combine was born.

It might not have occurred to the farm labourer that when the horse went he would be the next to be made redundant but the harvest field was transformed overnight when the combine harvester trundled in to cut the wheat. The rickyard was never needed again. Straw was set alight on the stubbles. The grain went into a drying plant and then into a silo, while the man in the cab – most always a contractor's man – visored and masked, pursued his solitary way, alone and remote from the very corn he was cutting.

The Corn Harvest

THE RED-LETTER DAY on the country calendar was always the cattle show, and not those more publicised events, the regional show and Smithfield, because the farther a countryman travelled the less likely he was to encounter people he knew. Even when the motorcar came on the scene and he could visit the agricultural show in the next county, and perhaps enter his prize milking cow to compete there in the dairy cattle class, he took less satisfaction in triumphing over someone he didn't know if he he had won a smaller prize at the local show.

This competitiveness applies in every branch of husbandry. The man with a good flock or a fine herd needs to know that it is as good as any he sees on his way to market. He takes a pride in his stock, his young gelding, his brood mare, his saddlebacks or his South Downs. When the local show is on he and his family, as well as his men, take a day off, dress themselves up and enjoy the occasion. A day at the show was something the stockman was always entitled to. The plough-man, when he was hired, needed to know the high days and holidays of his contract. He, like his master, looked forward to these occasions when they might spend the day hanging on a fence rail watching prize cattle being paraded, stallions with rosettes on their bridles, jaunty little ponies trotting by the side of their proud young owners, and mountainous, white-faced Hereford bulls being led less ceremoniously by the rings in their noses.

The term cattle show, which covered it all half a century ago, became in-adequate when mechanisation came to replace all the old-fashioned ways of cultivating land, for now the makers of implements insisted on having their corner and displaying their wares. Everything the forward-looking farmer might need, and a lot of things he had little use for, was suddenly there on the five or six acres of the show field along with the free lunch and the beer tent. Who could complain if the day lasted longer? The beer was free to anyone who looked a likely customer and a lot who didn't.

No farmer ever likes to think he has the reputation of being behind the times. The show is where he discovers tomorrow's world, listens to his friends, falls for the spiel of the salesman, and buys the new machine. How much more enlightened he is than his poor old grandfather who wouldn't have bought that crawling juggernaut because he knew there was no future in such machines.

Cattle Shows

T HE STAPLE DIET of the majority of people today may be a fast food of some kind: frozen beefburgers, fish-fingers, and chips. Without doubt the potato figures prominently in the diet of not just the Irish, but the people of the British Isles as a whole. The statistician may have graphs to show that bread, sliced or unsliced, is consumed in greater quantity than the frozen chip or the washed and scrubbed potato the supermarket sells, but the humble potato will surely hold its own, fresh from the earth, or processed until it makes the denizens of outer space fall about laughing.

It is a crop that can be grown in almost any kind of ground and, while there are extensive acreages devoted to it in different parts of the country, and early and even out-of-season potatoes are flown in from Mediterranean countries, there are literally thousands of tonnes of potatoes grown on small fields and parts of fields. The potato-grower of the fens has machinery for spinning the potato out of the furrow and grading it by size before it is mechanically bagged for the market. A man with a few furrows digs his potatoes with the old-fashioned, broad-tined potato fork. The small farmer may have a potato-digger that will spin out the crop leaving the tubers on the surface to be gathered by potato-pickers engaged by the day. This, in fact, was the way even quite large potato fields were harvested at the beginning of the present century. After corn harvest was safely carted and under thatch, the potato field waited for the potato-pickers. They might be the harvesters who had helped get the oats or wheat in, or gypsies who turned up every year to engage in an operation less arduous than lifting swedes.

In autumn the potato haulms are wilted and brown. The purple-mauve blossom is long forgotten. Partridges dustbath along the furrows. Crows hang about to peck the exposed green tuber. The sun is warm, the scene a mellow one, and the furrows easily broken by the digger, drawn once upon a time by a single horse but now hauled by the tractor. There is nothing quite so satisfying as to unearth a potato from the furrow, put it in a bucket and carry the gathering to the sack at the end of the row. A kind of timelessness prevails. It seems that this was the way of things centuries ago. The potato-picker is in tune with all his peasant ancestors.

The Potato Field

URDLE-MAKING as a country craft must go back to a distant past when the shepherd ceased to be an itinerant flockmaster, walking on and on with his sheep following him, as they do to this day in some parts of the eastern Mediterranean. In northern parts of Britain the shepherd in the hills constructed solid and permanent folds for his flock from the stone that lay all around him, and in these he contrived to bring his ewes through the lambing or sheared them in due season. In the rolling Downland as there is no stone to be quarried and carted and, since hazel grew in abundance in woodland areas, the trade of the hurdle-maker flourished.

The great advantage to the flockmaster was that he could move his pens and fold his flock on whatever part of the grazing seemed best in the light of the weather in a particular year. The movable pen allowed a flock to be divided, manipulated, and fed on fresh ground when a particular area had become too trodden or over-manured. The hurdle-maker, well-acquainted with the shepherd's needs made his hurdle light, roughly three feet in height and six feet long. In order to keep them upright the framework incorporated holes into which pointed poles were inserted and driven into the ground. The flockmaster needed an ample supply of wattled sections to enable him to hold his flock in one place while he prepared a new pen for them perhaps a few hundred yards away. The hurdles were made where the coppice wood grew and, since only comparatively mature hazel would serve his purpose, the hurdle-maker had to have a considerable area of coppice available to him to keep him supplied with raw material. His hands and wrists needed to be very strong to enable him to turn and interweave the split rod through his framework of uprights standing on a basic spar or jig with holes evenly spaced along its length to ensure that every hurdle was of exactly the same dimension. Because the split hazel was twisted and turned back round the outer stave, the final appearance of the hurdle was bark on one side and unbarked, split hazel on the other.

In addition to his work for shepherds the hurdle-maker still at the trade today occasionally finds a market for his wares when someone needs a stop-gap in a fence or gateway. Elsewhere the electric fence and the metal pen that can be transported in a truck may spell the end for one of our ancient country crafts.

Hurdles for the Shepherd

ORRIS DANCING and the folklore attached to many rituals seen in different parts of the country, where groups of men in outlandish garb solemnly dance their dances and recite their ancient rhymes, are part of the traditional entertainment enjoyed in villages, and around the village green, for as long as man can remember. Gartered and gaitered, these well-disguised country lads trip to and fro to the music of a mandolin or hurdy-gurdy while the rest of the village stares in wonder, laughs outright and applauds the more outrageous behaviour of individual members of the group. The Caesars gave the citizens of Rome their circus, but in the quiet villages of rural England the people provided their own.

Experts on the folklore and the customs observed in different parishes are often able to give plausible explanations of the ritual, the blacking of faces, the pattern of the dance, the superstitions involved, and the money demanded by the leader of the party of those appointed to collect dues from onlookers. The whole business is tribal. People not only love to be entertained on the village green or along the village street. They enjoy being awed, a little bewitched and frightened by it all, even when they know the mime and those performing, however well-disguised they may be. The performers hide behind the characters they are playing and are no longer themselves. This, too, is a kind of witchcraft. Such occasions are never entirely serious. The public loves to laugh and dance, just as the children of the village love the maypole, and the vicar must turn his blind eye on what is blatantly pagan, for doesn't he have the church decorated with the evergreen, holly and mistletoe at Christmas? Puritans finally put their foot down on morris men and their dancing, but in Henry VIII's reign it was part of the May festival in every rural parish. Morris dancers danced, rode the wooden hobby horse, and brandished sticks to the delight of those who had supped ale or mead and were briefly allowed respite in their serfdom.

The banning of the dance interrupted a pageant that had been introduced to Britain, it is said, by Edward I's queen. Thereafter it languished in obscurity until in our century there has been a great revival, with Morris dancing teams, schooled by enthusiastic members of the English Folk Dance Society, touring not only villages, but towns, to interest the general public in something that is part of our heritage. One result has been the formation of clubs and societies that compete with one another every year. Traditional things die hard, it is said, and dancing on the green dies hardest of all.

Dancing on the Green

TIME WAS WHEN ROOKERIES were found in closer proximity to human habitation than they are now. Rooks seemed to like living close to man. They built in elm trees more than in any other sort of tree and, being gregarious by nature, they built close to one another, renovating the old nests in early spring, quarrelling over sticks as well as the nests themselves, and generally behaving in a way not unlike the inhabitants of the hamlet below. People lived with the clamour and had superstitions concerning the rooks, when they seemed to build high or low, or when they deserted a rookery and left a village ominously quiet.

Dutch elm disease came along and the old elms died. Very often the rooks detected the disease before diagnosis by the county official whose job it was to condemn an affected elm and have it felled. The rookery moved to another clump of trees, perhaps a mile away, and with only a solitary cottage or farmstead for company; but, where elms were lacking and the disease had deprived the birds of their favourite tree, hedgerow rookeries, with nests much nearer the ground than hitherto were to be found in willows, or even in firwoods quite remote from human dwellings. The habits of the rehabilitated rooks didn't change. They had their battles and squabbles. They fought, tumbled earthwards, and flew back to perch in high branches and complain, and every morning in the spring they departed in a happy throng, a cheerfully cawing tribe of rooks in search of a rootfield or cornfield. The rook is the most engaging member of the crow family because of his gregariousness. He can also be one of the greatest pests to a farmer with newly sown wheat or rows of young turnips. The rook pulls plants, one after another, but to no avail. The rook exacts a toll a farmer simply isn't prepared to pay. Even before the young wheat is colouring the field a lovely soft green he puts down his minute gun to frighten away foraging rooks. A little later on comes the rook shoot, a relentless slaughter of the half-fledged rooks perched round the nests in surviving rookeries. It is a bloody business. Hundreds of rooks are killed all over the country, the meat of their breasts made into rook pie.

Rooks and Rookeries

KATING, IT IS SAID, had its origin with Norsemen who fashioned bone skates which they lashed to their feet in order to travel comfortably on frozen lakes and rivers. Whether or not these primitive skates were the real prototype of the wood and metal skates imported from the low countries centuries later, skating was fashionable when lakes and fens were frozen. The river Thames didn't freeze over often enough, but the lake in St James's Park was known to freeze over on occasion and fashionable people liked to be seen on the ice. The fens of East Anglia freeze more often, but nevertheless outdoor skating events have always been characterised by a certain spontaneity. For all of two hundred years the freeze has brought the people of Norfolk and Lincolnshire out to enjoy the spectacle, whether they are proficient skaters or possess no skates at all.

On these occasions the spectators stand and stare or slip and slide, breath steaming, their hands warmed by slapping their ribs. The experienced skaters glide here and there, swinging their arms professionally as they make tentative starts and short dashes along a wilderness of frost-petrified reeds. The All-England event waits upon the season and the weather. It cannot be ringed a month in advance on the country calendar. For all their sophisticated equipment weathermen can't predict when the fen will freeze from a fragile picture-glass thickness to one that will bear the weight of a couple skating with their arms linked. The frozen fen belongs to everybody. The expert has practised elsewhere. The novice, strapping on his father's old Dutch or Swedish skates, wobbles out, falls and gets to his feet again to dust the frost from his clothes and reminds himself that he must keep out of the way of those conceited, completely co-ordinated people from the indoor rinks. The enchantment lies in the fact that this is a natural, outdoor experience, without floodlighting or canned music. Painters and engravers have always taken a delight in capturing the scene on canvas and paper. It has the nostalgic magic of a Dickensian Christmas card.

It is the cold wind from the North Sea that dulls the enthusiasm of spectators in the end. Elderly men stamp their feet and warm themselves with a nip from a flask. Mothers stand patiently waiting for their red-faced children to have had enough. This is a winter to be remembered, a kind of Lowry picture, carried in the mind, long after the last of the skaters has come off the ice with frost in crystals on his woolly hat and his cheeks and nose quite blue.

Fen Skaters

N COUNTLESS VILLAGES dotted about rural England, often on a Sunday, and less frequently on Saturday, during summer, the sound of a bat hitting a cricket ball indicates that the English game is in progress. Village cricket is a very parochial and partisan affair, and something quite different from the kind of entertainment at Lords or on the sun-scorched pitches of Australia, India or Jamaica. Little has changed in a century so far as the village game is concerned. The spectators may be counted in tens on special occasions, never in hundreds. The atmosphere is friendly. Almost always the competing sides know one another by their first names. Competitiveness may result in a few hard words, but no one needs to wear body armour, and no one is ever carried off to hospital after failing to cope with a bouncer. The club secretary and his wife concern themselves with refreshment and perhaps the scoreboard. Appeals against the light are infrequent. Umpires may have to take a little more criticism than those on the county ground, but they are used to it. They are somehow expected to be biased and partisan. Matches are won and lost by the umpire, and even when he is a veritable Solomon arguments go on about his decision or lack of decision when the day is over, and shadows are gathering along the village street and on the green.

It all began roughly two centuries ago, though the game was played in Surrey, it is said, in the middle of the seventeenth century. Hambledon Cricket Club was formed in 1750. It continued for more than forty years until it was disbanded and Marylebone Cricket Club took charge of the game, finally moving to Lords in 1814. Village cricket has thriven wherever a side can be mustered. It is as much a feature of village life as the parochial church council, the parish council or the Women's Institute. It depends on the butcher, the baker, the candlestick-maker, the vicar and the postman who play year after year, enjoying not just the rivalry that exists between their own and the neighbouring village, but the whole social occasion, the bonhomie, the arguments in the bar after the match – something that is in the tradition of village life.

The village green, the church and the pub wouldn't be the same if the village couldn't field a side and keep up that tradition. Is it cricket, people ask, when the pitch is laid out on the very place where the bonfire was built, when boundaries are doubtful and lounging spectators get in the way? Would it be quite the same with everyone in whites and a computer scoreboard to keep tally?

The Village Green and Cricket

 HERE IS, THE BIBLE tells us, a time to reap and a time to sow, and in spring when most things are sown and planted the birds invariably take their toll. Rooks, crows, pigeons and even gamebirds follow the sower and the seed drill, picking grain that hasn't been covered by harrowing and rolling, or scratching to unearth the seed lovingly covered by the drill. In times long gone the sower strode the ploughed land as the great masters portrayed him, broadcasting corn with a deft movement of one hand after another, as evenly as any present-day mechanical device can spread grain. The sower's stride was even, his rhythm perfect, or the corn would come up in bunches and there would be bare patches on the cultivated field. As surely as the sower sowed, the crows came sweeping in to feast on the grain, and small boys were employed as scarecrows, banging tins and rushing about to drive the birds away. Sometimes the human scarecrow would be armed with a muzzle-loader with which he could shoot a crow, and hang it on a stick to draw in more of the clamorous and indignant crow tribe to be shot when the gun was, once again, loaded and primed.

The sower was a rare individual in the rural community. Few men had the pace, the stature, the rhythm that was required, and to overcome this some rustic genius invented a little machine that came to be known as a fiddle. It was operated by a bow attached to a string that turned a wheel designed to scatter corn with which the fiddle was loaded. 'Fiddling' his way over the ploughed field, the farmer could sow his own corn and not have to wait in line for the sower. On the cornfield he put up a scarecrow of straw and wood dressed in some of his own old clothes, his human scarecrow was now armed with a double-barrelled shotgun to bag woodpigeons and crows, though both species are very wary birds. Time marched on, and the seed drill made the fiddle obsolete. The old straw and wood scarecrow was made redundant by the employment of a mechanical one with a time fuse that allowed an explosion to take place at regular intervals during the day. The birds became used to this machine, and even the kind of minute gun that took its place, and the last resort would seem to be an 'inflatable man' who rears up from the field and puts crows and pigeons to flight immediately. This, one might think, could be the ultimate deterrent, but who can say?

The Sowers Field

ARES, UNLIKE RABBITS, come under the game laws. They are traditional animals of the chase, only to be hunted by the owner of the land and those to whom he may assign his right. In some parts of the country they have always been numerous and regarded as pests by farmers with little interest in the cultivation of game and shooting rights. Hare shoots are the order of the day in places overrun with hares, but the sporting gent has a strong aversion to wanton slaughter of hares and would have them hunted by hounds, coursed, or pursued by a pack of deep-chested, short-legged, bustling beagles.

Coursing with greyhounds is not the most efficient way of catching a hare. the greyhound, fast as any other hunting hound, overruns its quarry, and the hare, wise in the art of survival, turns abruptly while the wretched greyhound, bewildered, looks about to discover where the hare has gone. The coursers have to cooperate with their charges to make sure that the hares are funnelled into a narrow avenue down which the hound can give chase. Beagles hunt like foxhounds, but, with shorter legs, bustle and fuss more, and mill round hillocks of gorse and bracken, taking the scent, bundling on and sometimes streaming off after a hare long gone through the next hedge and over the hill. The beagle would probably run himself into the ground if the hare kept running straight for the distant pastures and the next parish, but the hare is no more able to do this than a trout that darts upstream only to turn about and seek cover under the bank where he was first accosted. Hares belong in their own small parish. Like the fox, they know the ground. When they are driven out of familiar places they don't know the escape routes. The master of the beagle pack knows the hill or the hollow where he has put up a hare for years and he knows, of course, that the startled hare will run in a circle and come back to the place on which he was born. Their dawdling in the bushes brought to an end by the huntsman and his assistants, the beagle pack trundles on to follow the hare round and round the fields.

Kills are hardly more frequent than in fox-hunting. The exercise is to display the ability of hounds to follow scent, something those who would condemn all hunting out of hand may never understand. Most hares that hang on the dealer's rail died in a more violent exercise.

Hare Hunting

has been set in Monotype Van Dijck, named after the famous seventeeth-century Dutch punchcutter Christoffel Van Dyck. Although it remains unclear whether the type was originally cut by Christoffel, his son Abraham, or was merely a part of the stock of the Van Dyck typefoundry in Amsterdam, it is certain that it *was* a distinguished and famous type in its day and is certainly among the most successful of the Monotype Corporation's revivals. Notable for its small proportioned capitals, its graceful (and in some cases blatantly eccentric) italic, and its very fine hairlines, it remains among the loveliest and most delicate of the seventeenth century 'classical' faces.

The engravings by Christopher Wormell were cut in the end grain of boxwood with a burin. This venerable technique was perfected by the Englishman Thomas Bewick in the late eighteenth century and enables an artist of Mr. Wormell's talents to render precise detail and nuance with astonishing accuracy. In his work (and his art), Mr. Wormell follows directly in this English pastoral tradition begun by Bewick and continued in this century by engravers like Reynolds Stone, Ian Stephens, Howard Phipps, and George Tute.